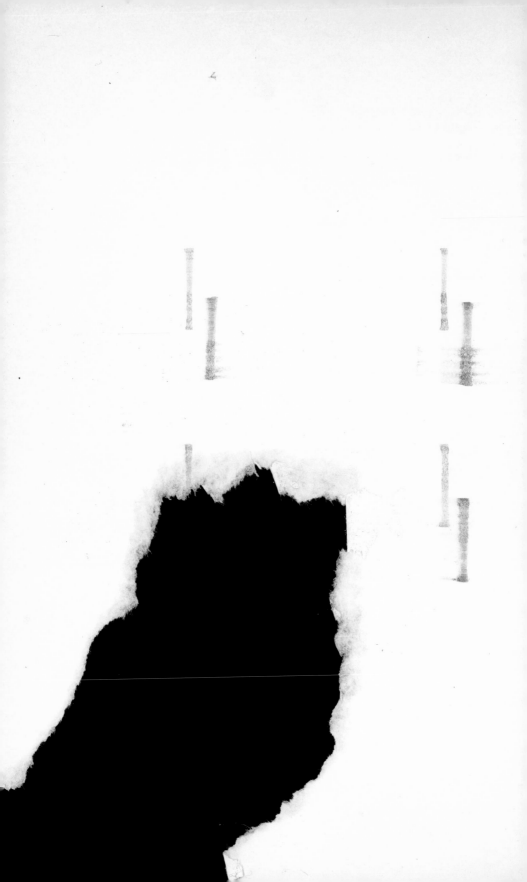

CAREERS IN PHYSICAL REHABILITATION THERAPY

CAREERS IN PHYSICAL REHABILITATION THERAPY

By Halima Touré

A Career
Concise Guide

FRANKLIN WATTS
NEW YORK | LONDON | 1977

Photographs courtesy of:

New York University Medical Center Institute of Rehabilitation Medicine: pp. 5, 11, 12, 14, 18, 26–27, 31, 33; The Burke Rehabilitation Center: pp. 20, 54, 59; Board of Education, City of New York: pp. 40, 44; The Lighthouse: p. 47.

Library of Congress Cataloging in Publication Data

Touré, Halima.
    Careers in physical rehabilitation therapy.

    (A Career concise guide)
    Includes index.
    SUMMARY: Discusses careers relating to physical rehabilitation. Includes physical, recreation, speech, and dance therapists, orthopedic surgeon, orientation instructor, and prosthetist.
    1. Physical therapy—Vocational guidance—Juvenile literature.   2. Occupational therapy—Vocational guidance—Juvenile literature. 3. Speech therapy—Vocational guidance—Juvenile literature. [1. Physical therapy—Vocational guidance.   2. Occupational therapy—Vocational guidance.   3. Speech therapy—Vocational guidance. 4. Teachers of the physically handicapped—Vocational guidance.   5. Vocational guidance] I. Title.
    RM701.T68   615'.82'023   77-7171
    ISBN 0-531-01306-5

Contents

Acknowledgments

The author wishes to express her gratitude to the
people at the following institutions who
graciously provided their assistance and cooperation:

Department of Physical Medicine and Rehabilitation
Veterans' Hospital
First Avenue and 24th Street
New York, N.Y.

The New York Association for the Blind (The Lighthouse)
111 E. 59th Street
New York, N.Y.

The New York League for the Hard of Hearing
71 W. 23rd Street
New York, N.Y.

Turtle Bay Music School Arts-In-Therapy Program
244 E. 52nd Street
New York, N.Y.

CAREERS IN PHYSICAL REHABILITATION THERAPY

Rehabilitation Careers

Several factors should be considered when deciding what career to pursue. In addition to considerations of income earned from the work and a sense of personal satisfaction, you may want to consider areas where you can render service to others. Many valuable experiences can be derived from careers in the field of physical rehabilitation through helping people overcome and/or adjust to disabilities resulting from accident or illness.

Many of you have no doubt viewed telethons soliciting funds for research and treatment of physically disabling diseases, such as cerebral palsy, cystic fibrosis, and muscular dystrophy. And while a person afflicted with the condition may be called on to represent those with the disease, the viewer is rarely shown what goes on to help that person function on a day-to-day basis with his or her disability.

There are numerous people involved in the rehabilitation process, people with varying skills designed to aid the patient in achieving a high degree of competence in certain tasks. Increasingly, the treatment of the physically disabled is being carried out on a team basis. That is, practitioners in different therapeutic disciplines work together to improve the level of health and functioning of the patient. The team usually is headed by a medical doctor. This could be a physiatrist, a physician who specializes in physical medicine and rehabilitation with emphasis on the different therapies available to heal the patient. Or the medical doctor could be one who is responsible for treating the patient and prescribing needed

[1]

rehabilitative services. Other members of the team include: the **Corrective Therapist.** This person uses physical education techniques in the rehabilitation process. The **Physical Therapist.** This worker must have knowledge of the body's musculature, the skeleton, the nervous system, and other physical processes. The knowledge allows the therapist to use exercises, water, heat, light, and other tools and techniques to strengthen, condition, and reeducate the body parts affected by illness or accident. The **Occupational Therapist.** This person helps the physically disabled to regain the ability to perform routine tasks or to adjust to an artificial limb. The **Prosthetist** and/or **Orthotist** designs and builds the braces and artificial limbs needed to foster maximum independence and mobility. The **Speech Pathologist** works with a person whose speech has been impaired through accident or illness or is the result of a congenital defect. The **Rehabilitation Counselor** counsels and advises the patient and his or her family on the job opportunities available for the disabled worker.

In addition to the above-mentioned members of the rehabilitation team, there are numerous other workers, both medical and nonmedical, whose skills are necessary supports to the entire rehabilitation process. The **Manual Arts Therapist,** the **Music, Art, and Dance Therapists,** and the **Recreation Therapists** provide services that augment and round out those provided by the core team.

This book describes each of a variety of job categories in this field, covering those requiring advanced degrees (physicians, therapists, et al.) as well as those obtainable with a high school diploma or its equivalent and those requiring two-year college or certificated programs. Also included in some instances are the personal attributes that would be helpful for the job, and a sampling of the kinds of courses that comprise the curriculum. The certifying or professional associations in each profession are listed at the end of each chapter. You may see yourself in one of these vocations.

The Physiatrist

The **Physiatrist** (fiz ē 'a trist) is a medical doctor who specializes in treating disabilities of the nervous, muscular, and skeletal systems. The physiatrist's job is to diagnose and evaluate the extent of the patient's disability and to prescribe the various therapies needed to help the patient tc function to the best of his/her capability. Often functioning as the head of a rehabilitation team, this medical specialist rarely makes the headlines with his/her achievements. The physiatrist's work with a young mother who has been left partially paralyzed as the result of an automobile accident does not provide the spectacular news copy of the surgeon involved in heart transplants. What the physiatrist does do, however, is attempt to harness all the knowledge and resources at his or her disposal to put back together a potentially shattered life. The specialist helps the injured woman to regain as much mobility as possible and to learn to function in her home and with her family in spite of her disability and to accept her limitations as much as possible.

The physiatrist may be involved in the initial care of the patient or may be called in after the acute phase of care is completed. The specialist must plan the nature of the chronic care that the patient will receive and build a rehabilitation team that may include one or all of the following: physical, occupational, recreational, corrective, art, dance, and music therapies, and vocational rehabilitation counseling. The patient is viewed as a total organism, and the parts that make up the whole are seen in relationship to one another. The physiatrist's choice of therapies includes those that provide healing for the psysiological, psychological, and social aspects of the patient, taking into account not only the broadest implications of the patient's disabilities but also the most minute—that is, how the injury or illness has affected the person's ability to tie shoelaces as well as the ability to earn a living. The physiatrist must also determine if artificial limbs or adoptive devices are necessary to achieve the greatest degree of self-sufficiency.

Once the physiatrist has prescribed the necessary therapies, he/she must constantly review the reports and evaluations of the rehabilitation team members, reexamine the patient at regular intervals to determine the effects of the treatment, and decide whether or not to change or discontinue a treatment. The specialist may also administer certain treatments to the patient.

Most physiatrists are employed in rehabilitation centers and other institutions that maintain departments of Physical Medicine and Rehabilitation. A small number work in private practice in large group settings.

The qualifications required to become a physiatrist include a bachelor's degree from an accredited college, and graduation from a medical school recognized by the Council on Medical Education and Hospitals of the Ameri-

A physiatrist monitoring the progress of a patient.

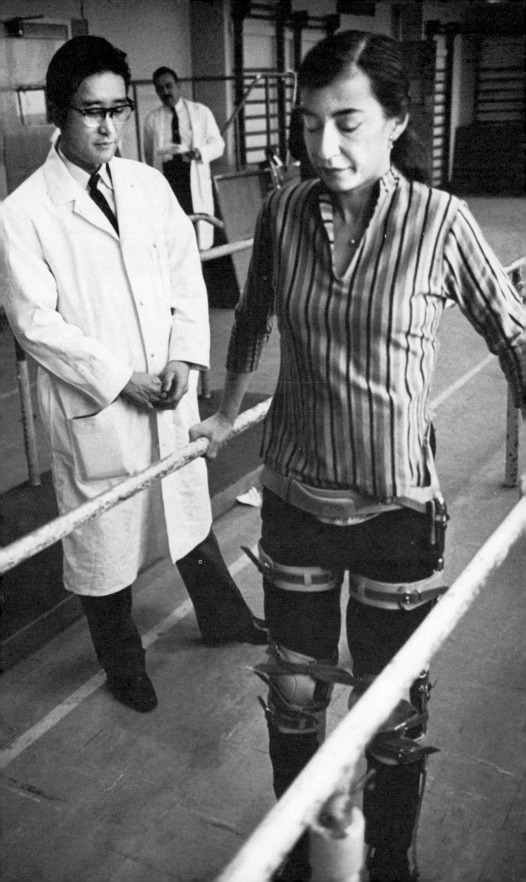

can Medical Association, or the Committee on Hospitals of the Bureau of Professional Education of the American Osteopathic Association; a license to practice medicine or osteopathy in the state where the candidate intends to work is also necessary. A residency in physical medicine and rehabilitation is desirable.

Note: There are seven colleges of osteopathic medicine accredited by the American Osteopathic Association. A bachelor's degree with course work in chemistry, biology, physics and English is the minimum entrance requirement.

For further information contact:

American Academy of Physical Medicine and Rehabilitation
30 North Michigan Avenue
Chicago, Ill. 60602

American Osteopathic Association
212 East Ohio Street
Chicago, Ill. 60611

In Canada contact:

Canadian Medical Association
P.O. Box 8650
Ottawa, Ont. K1G 0G8

Canadian Association of Physical Medicine and Rehabilitation
P.O. Box 8244
Ottawa, Ont. K1G 3H7

The Orthopedic Surgeon

The **Orthopedic Surgeon** is a medical doctor who specializes in surgery of the bones and joints that may be required because of congenital defects such as clubfoot or so-called "curvature of the spine," problems or possible deformities caused by fractures and dislocations, and disabilities of bones and joints resulting from infections.

Like the physiatrist's work, that of the orthopedic surgeon's is not the glamorous specialty that makes headlines. It's the quiet kind that can make the difference between life in a wheelchair or walking on one's own, hand joints rendered useless or functioning well enough to thread a needle.

Approximately 60 percent of the disabilities in the most recent wars were orthopedic in nature. When at peace, traffic accidents, athletic injuries, and congenital defects keep the percentage at wartime levels. The orthopedic surgeon treats wounds and injuries involving the extremities and spine, bone and joint diseases, flatfeet, torn cartilage of the knee, backaches, dislocations of the shoulder, and strains, sprains, and amputations. He/she is also responsible for the fitting of artificial limbs. Recent surgical innovations have widened the scope of orthopedics, which is now also concerned with the insertion of artificial joints, muscle transplants, and new techniques of hand surgery.

The orthopedic surgeon is often viewed as a high-class "mechanic" in the medical profession, with his or her work limited to bones and joints, but he/she must have a firm foundation in medicine as well as surgical experience. No part of the body can be viewed as a single entity—it must be viewed as part of a complex structure in which all the parts interrelate. In addition to performing skeletal and joint surgery, the orthopedist must be able to control any other medical conditions affecting the injury.

At present there is only one orthopedic surgeon for every 150,000 people. Training for the profession requires a bachelor's degree from an accredited university, graduation from an approved medical school, an internship, one year of surgical residency training, and three years of orthopedic surgery in an approved residency program. Upon completion of these requirements, the orthopedist is eligible to apply for the American Board of Orthopedic Surgery's two-part certifying exam. Although anyone who holds a state license to practice medicine may legally practice orthopedic surgery, certification is necessary to qualify for the better jobs.

Patients are usually referred to orthopedic surgeons by family or other physicians. Surgeons are employed by Veterans Administration and other hospitals, the Federal Crippled Children's Bureau, and in private practice.

For further information contact:

American Orthopedic Association
430 N. Michigan Avenue
Chicago, Ill. 60611

In Canada contact:

Canadian Orthopaedic Association
5470 Queen Mary Road, Suite 1
Montreal, Quebec, Canada H3X 1V6

Canadian Medical Association
P.O. Box 8650
Ottawa, Ont. K1G 0G8

The Physical Therapist

The **Physical Therapist,** also referred to as a physio-therapist, is a significant member of the rehabilitation team. Her (most physical therapists thus far have been women) job involves working with patients who are disabled by illness or accident or who were born with a handicap. She usually works with the patient's physician to evaluate the extent of the disability by performing and analyzing certain tests. She is concerned with the neuromuscular, musculoskeletal, sensorimotor, and related cardiovascular and respiratory functions. Using the test results as a basis, the physical therapist, among other things, plans a program of therapy designed to reeducate muscles and increase strength, endurance, and coordination. She also teaches the patient how to use a device such as an artificial limb or a brace (known as a prosthesis or orthosis). She (or he) uses various kinds of equipment: exercise tables, stationary bicycles, walkers, wheelchairs, practice stairs, parallel bars, and pulleys and weights. Heat and cold, sound and water are used to relieve pain and alter a physiological condition.

The therapist herself must be in good physical condition, for the work can be physically demanding. She sometimes must lift and carry equipment, supplies, and materials weighing up to fifty pounds. She usually has mechnical devices or other personnel to help move heavier equipment. The job calls for much stooping, pushing, and pulling when moving patients or equipment into position for treatment, as well as handling and manipulating when giving massages.

[9]

The therapist must keep written records of treatment given and the results, as well as patient reactions that will be referred to by other members of the rehabilitation team. She also must communicate verbally with medical personnel, the patients, and oftentimes their relatives. Therefore she must have a good command of written and spoken standard English.

While the work itself is very physical, much mental and creative ability is required in the education and training. A strong aptitude in the sciences is highly recommended, for the curriculum leading to a bachelor of science in physical therapy includes such courses as anatomy, physiology, neurology, and biology.

Physical therapy commands a professional status and any practitioner on this level is regulated by law. The license to practice is granted in each state according to its legal requirements. Examinations are given at least once a year. The Board of Medical Examiners in the particular state will supply information regarding licensing requirements and procedures.

Physical therapists work in a variety of settings including departments of physical therapy in general or specialized hospitals, schools for crippled children, long-term-care hospitals and nursing homes for the chronically ill or elderly, rehabilitation centers, community and governmental agencies providing health services, and in colleges and universities offering educational programs in physical therapy. The field covers a wide range of activities such as direct patient care, con-

A physical therapist teaching an amputee to strengthen the muscles that will control his prosthesis.

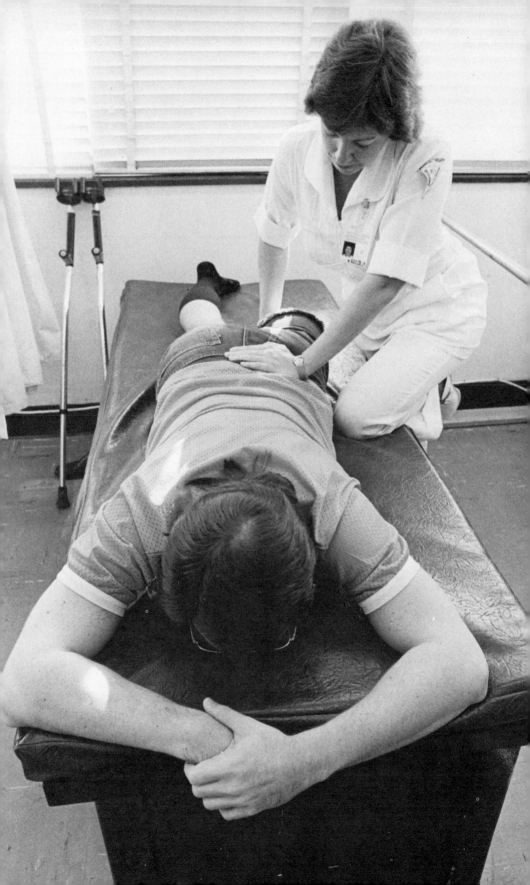

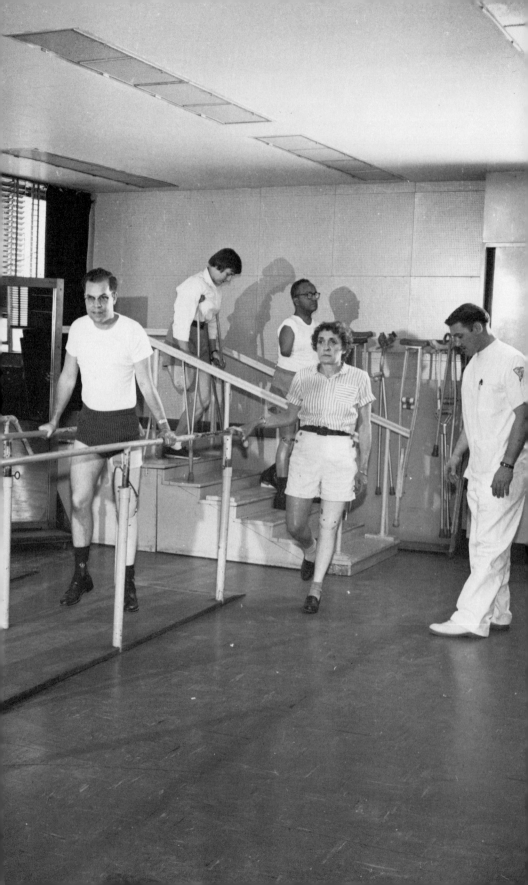

sultation, supervision, teaching, administration, research, and community service.

There are several paths a student can take that lead to professional qualification in physical therapy. The bachelor's degree program in an approved college or university requires four years for completion. The curriculum consists of the general college courses, basic health science and clinical science courses, and an internship under supervision of about four months' duration that provides practical experience in the field. Students who select a major other than physical therapy but closely related to it (physical education, for example) may enter a program that awards a certificate upon successful completion. The course generally takes twelve to sixteen months. Certain science requirements may need to be met for admission to such a program. Graduates of these programs are considered just as qualified as graduates of the bachelor's degree programs. Holders of bachelor's degrees in a related field also can enter a two-year master's degree program. Upon receipt of the degree, the graduate is able to enter a teaching, supervisory, or administrative position.

PHYSICAL THERAPY ASSISTANT

Those students who for one reason or another are unable to complete a four-year college program but who are interested in the field of physical therapy can study for two years to become **Physical Therapy Assistants.** The

A physical therapist conducting
an amputee ambulation program.
Modern prosthetic services include
not only the fitting of the artificial
limb, but also instructions in its use.

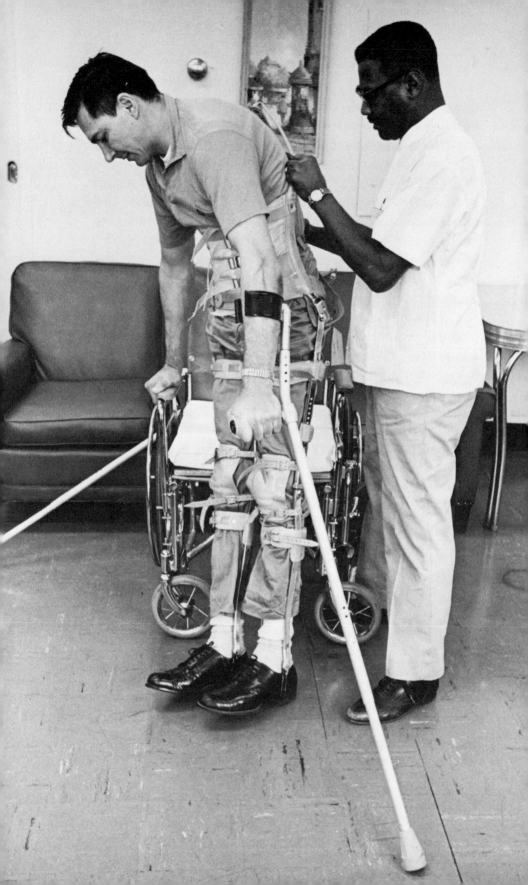

assistant is a skilled technical health worker who assists the therapist in carrying out the treatment programs. Programs for physical therapy assistants are located in the community or junior college. The course of study includes biological, physical, and social sciences, as well as the humanities and technical physical therapy courses and practical experience. Many states require that a physical therapy assistant be licensed for employment.

PHYSICAL THERAPY AIDE

For students who do not plan to attend college, a position as a **Physical Therapy Aide** may be worth investigating. An aide must be at least eighteen years old and must complete an on-the-job training program in a hospital or clinical facility. The physical therapy aide's primary duty is to carry out certain routine jobs connected with the operation of the physical therapy service, but he/she may assist in some patient-related activities working under the supervision of the physical therapist. If you are interested in such a position, contact the chief physical therapist or personnel director of your local hospital.

For further information contact:

American Physical Therapy Association
1156 15th Street, N.W.
Washington, D.C. 20005

In Canada contact:

Canadian Physiotherapy Association
25 Imperial St.
Toronto, Ont. M5P 1B9

**A physical therapy aide
helping a braced paraplegic
get into his wheelchair.**

The Occupational Therapist

Another member of the rehabilitation team is the **Occupational Therapist,** whose primary role is to plan and carry out activities that help patients perform the tasks of daily living with their particular injury or physical disability. The therapist is concerned with helping the patient to adjust to his or her handicap and to become as self-sufficient as possible.

The occupational therapist might teach a housewife who has lost a hand in an accident how to clean and clothe herself, how to cook and clean her house. She/he might teach weaving to a person afflicted with arthritis in the fingers, a task that would help to exercise the fingers and might also have vocational significance. She/he may design mechanical devices that will assist disabled persons in their daily functioning. One occupational therapist, inspired by a sandwich holder made for severely afflicted cerebral palsy patients, designed a "napkin holder" shaped device of plexiglass that can be used by anyone who can control the head and trunk somewhat but cannot hold or place the sandwich in the mouth. It is attached to two suction cups which allow it to be used vertically or horizontally.

There is room for a great deal of creativity in occupational therapy. The therapist has at his/her disposal such manual arts as woodworking, metalworking, arts and crafts, and other activities from which to plan a program. The therapist must use her/his knowledge and powers of observation to determine what activities are useful for a particular person with a particular disability—how much time will be needed to accomplish the task, what goals to set for individual patients, and when to replace one activity with another, as well as when to add an activity to build the patient's endurance. These decisions are not made alone because the occupational therapist is part of a team of practitioners concerned with various aspects of the patient, but the therapist must be able to make evaluations and recommendations from her/his own viewpoint in addition to carrying out the other prescriptions or recommendations for therapy.

To prepare for a career as an occupational therapist you must successfully complete a four-year college course with a bachelor of science degree in occupational therapy. The curriculum consists of such science courses as biology and anatomy and others that teach the structure of the human body and body systems and the human growth process. The student also studies sociology, psychology, and other courses dealing with the human development process, developmental tasks and needs in various phases of life, and the meaning of activity in the development of human potential and competence. Knowledge of health and the effects of illness are taught in courses describing birth defects, the effects of various diseases, and the causes, development, and management of physical, emotional, and environmental stresses and trauma. Courses in occupational theory and practice round out the curriculum, with a minimum of six months of supervised field experience required.

If the student majors in a field other than occupational therapy and decides after graduation that he/she would like to prepare for the field, a two-year graduate program leading to a master of science degree in oc-

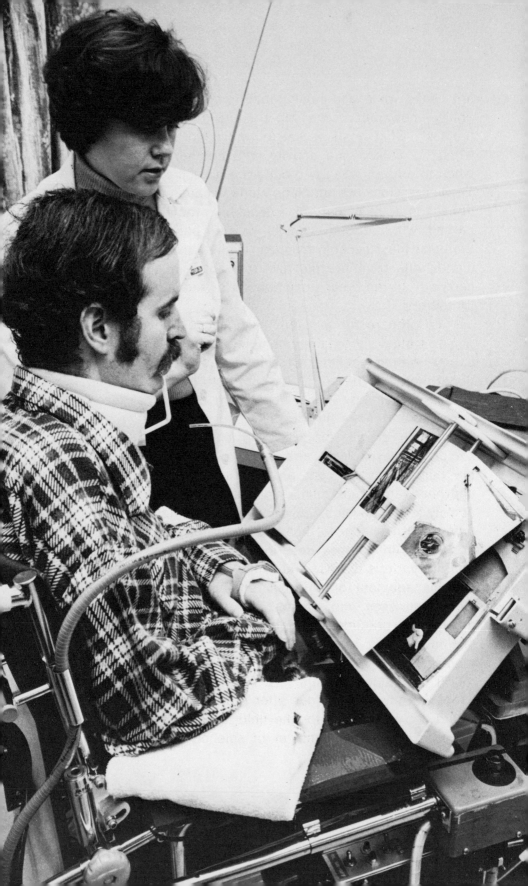

cupational therapy is available. Some programs offer certificates of proficiency in the field and may be less than two years.

Ph.D. degree programs exist for those who might want to teach, enter research, or aspire to administrative positions.

Good verbal and writing skills are required to function well as an occupational therapist, for you must communicate with patients and doctors, understand medical terminology, and keep written progress and evaluation reports for the patients you serve.

Employment opportunities exist in hospitals and clinics, rehabilitation and long-term-care facilities, sheltered workshops, schools and camps, private homes, housing projects, and community agencies and centers.

The American Occupational Therapy Association gives a national registration examination for graduates in occupational therapy. Those who qualify are entitled to use the designation Registered Occupational Therapist (O.T.R.).

OCCUPATIONAL THERAPY ASSISTANT

Another avenue into the field is as an **Occupational Therapy Assistant,** who works under the supervision of the Registered Occupational Therapist and assists him or her in carrying out the treatment program that has been designed by the O.T.R. You may qualify for such a po-

An occupational therapist showing a quadraplegic how to use the "huff and puff" breathing device. This device activates a motor that turns the book page.

[19]

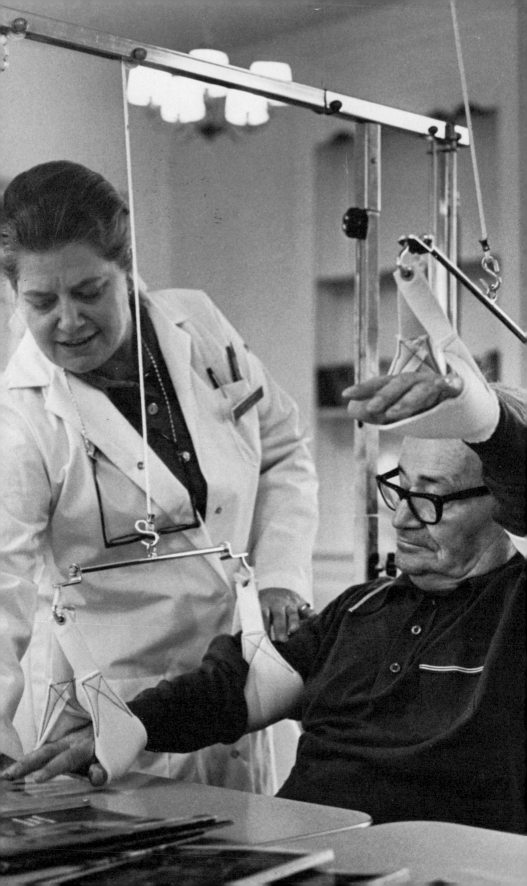

sition following completion of a two-year program in occupational therapy, leading to the associate in applied science degree, at an accredited junior or community college. Some institutions offer a one-year certificate program, and some hospitals have their own 20- or 25-week certificate programs. The latter usually are open only to people working in the sponsoring hospital. The American Occupational Therapy Association offers certification to those who have completed one of the above-mentioned courses and passed the national certification examination. Successful candidates are entitled to use the designation Certified Occupational Therapy Assistant (C.O.T.A.).

OCCUPATIONAL THERAPY AIDE

Some may enter the field as **Occupational Therapy Aides.** Requirements for such a position include a high school or equivalency diploma with some knowledge of the subjects to be taught to patients, such as industrial arts and homemaking, including sewing, or a working knowledge of a craft or hobby. Some hospital experience is desirable, but the methods and procedures of the work are taught on the job. The aide works under the supervision of the occupational therapist.

For further information contact:

American Occupational Therapy Association
6000 Executive Boulevard, Suite 200
Rockville, Md. 20852

**An occupational therapy
assistant at work**

In Canada contact:

Canadian Association of Occupational Therapists
Suite M19
4 New Street
Toronto, Ont. M5R 1P6

The Corrective Therapist

The distinguishing feature of the **Corrective Therapist's** job is the use of physical education methods and techniques to treat specific disabilities. The corrective therapist provides a program of physical exercise and activities that have been prescribed by a physician. He/she uses orthopedic equipment, standard gymnasium equipment, and gymnasium equipment that has been adapted to be used by disabled persons. The therapist uses basic motor learning principles to teach developmental movement, and teaches postural alignment and bodily movement by reeducating the impaired muscles and nerves. He/she also teaches sports and games that have been adapted to the playing capabilities of the disabled and handicapped. Upon recommendation by a physician, the therapist can employ his/her particular expertise in caring for and treating individuals suffering from heart, circulation, and respiratory disorders, neurological and sensory disorders, mental retardation, and acute, chronic, and congenital conditions of the nerve, muscle, and skeletal systems.

Additionally, the therapist may demonstrate to patients the use, function, and care of braces, artificial limbs, and other devices designed to assist in walking, and teach amputees and partially paralyzed patients techniques for walking and the use of specially equipped automobiles.

Students with a high aptitude for sports and physical education might want to add this job category to possible career choices.

The education needed to qualify is four years of college leading to a bachelor's degree, with a major in physical education, plus four hundred hours of clinical experience under proper supervision and approved by the American Corrective Therapy Association.

The association confers certification, and candidates seeking certification must be active members of the association. Candidates who have met the internship requirement and who have a bachelor's degree in physical education are eligible to take the certification examination, which consists of written, oral, and demonstration sections. After passing the exam, the designation Certified Corrective Therapist may be used. Certification may be necessary for employment. Corrective therapists usually are employed in hospitals and rehabilitation centers.

For further information contact:

American Corrective Therapy Association
c/o Mr. James LaSasso, Secretary
Corrective Therapy Department
Veterans Administration Hospital
Long Beach, California

The Manual Arts Therapist

This job title exists only in Veterans' Administration Hospitals. Students with a talent for and interest in the industrial arts—metalworking, woodworking, electricity, graphic and applied arts, and agriculture—may wish to investigate a career as a **Manual Arts Therapist.** This job consists of planning and administering manual arts activities that the patients' physicians have deemed beneficial in their treatment. The activities oftentimes have some vocational significance to the disabled person. They can help him or her maintain or improve work skills or develop new work skills adapted to his or her disability.

The manual arts therapist consults with other members of the rehabilitation team in planning and organizing the work activities. He/she attempts to set up actual work situations in the hospital building or on the grounds to instill self-confidence and to determine if a patient can perform in a real-life situation. For example, the therapist may have a radio and television repair shop set up where the disabled person is required to put in a certain amount of time on certain tasks. Patients who are physically able may manage a garden plot on the grounds or manage the lawn, trees, and shrubbery. The therapist instructs the patients in the technical aspects of the work and in the use and care of tools and equipment.

The therapist also must prepare reports showing the development of the patient's tolerance for work and his emotional and social adjustments to the situation to aid medical personnel in determining the patient's progress and ability to meet the physical and mental demands of employment.

In order to become a manual arts therapist, completion of a four-year program at an accredited college or university is required. A major in manual arts therapy is recommended, although a major in industrial arts, teacher education, industrial education, or agriculture is acceptable. In addition, the student must complete a clinical training program of about six months supervised by a physician at an accredited college or university that is affiliated with a hospital or rehabilitation center. A master's degree in manual arts therapy may be required for advancement or for administrative or teaching positions.

Generally, manual arts therapists are employed in hospitals, rehabilitation centers, sheltered workshops, and special schools for handicapped students.

At present there is no certification, registration, or licensing required to practice in this field.

For further information contact:

American Association for Rehabilitation Therapy
P.O. Box 93
North Little Rock, Ark. 72116

The Recreation Therapist

The **Recreation Therapist** focuses on the activities that fill the patient's leisure time during long recovery periods or during the rehabilitation process. When illness and/or disabilities occur, the afflicted person's life

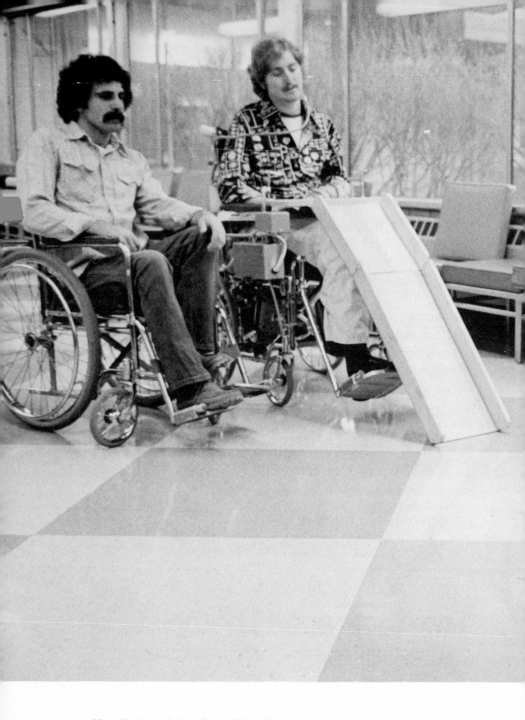

**Handicapped bowlers. That they
are now active is the result of
working with a recreation therapist.**

is disrupted in all areas, but many of the needs still remain. The need for recreational activities is met by the recreation therapist (or therapeutic recreation specialist), who plans and directs games, adapted sports, hobbies, and other social activities made available to the patients.

The recreation therapist is often part of the rehabilitation team and patients are referred to him or her for an activity or activities prescribed by the physician in charge. The therapist then introduces the activity—for arts or crafts or dramatics—and adapts it to the patient's capabilities.

Ken Gilchrist is in charge of recreation therapy in a Veterans Hospital. In addition to the duties with individual patients, Ken also is responsible for planning and overseeing the recreational activities for the entire hospital. Aided by a staff of four therapists, he schedules weekly feature film showings, coordinates volunteer groups who provide Bingo games, a mobile library, and a variety of other services, plans daily or weekend excursions in the summer for mobile patients, directs the music therapist's activities, and programs celebrities, variety shows, and other entertainment offerings.

Ken and his staff feel that they need more people to do the job the way they believe it ought to be done. Ken thinks more time needs to be spent with individuals and small groups of patients in recreation counseling. Many disabled and handicapped people need help in re-thinking how they will use their leisure and recreational time once they return to their home situations. However, staff increases in recreation therapy departments often are placed far down on the priority list when purse strings are tightened. Also, recreation therapists often find themselves in conflicting schedules with the other therapies, such as physical, occupational, corrective, manual arts, etc., and all are vying unintentionally for the patients' time. Most facilities that have a recreation therapy department, though, recognize its value in the rehabilitation process.

Educational requirements for a recreational therapist's job include a bachelor's degree in recreation therapy or recreation leadership with an emphasis on rehabilitation. If you wish to move into administration, teaching, or training others, a master's degree program with special emphasis on therapeutic recreation is recommended.

Recreation therapists are employed in VA hospitals, correctional facilities, special schools, and community recreation centers.

For further information contact:

National Therapeutic Recreation Society
1601 North Kent Street
Arlington, Va. 22209

The Prosthetist and Orthotist

The **Prosthetist** and **Orthotist** are the members of the rehabilitation team who are concerned with producing mechanical aids, such as artificial limbs and braces, for the disabled person. The prosthetist works from the physician's prescription to design, fabricate, and fit the artificial limb to an amputee. The orthotist designs, fabricates, and fits orthopedic braces, called orthoses, which are used to support parts of the body that have been weakened by birth defects, disease, or accident. A person may be both an orthotist and a prosthetist, but many people choose only one area in which to work.

What, exactly, does the job entail? First, a doctor refers a patient to the prosthetist/orthotist. In consultation with the prosthetist/orthotist, the physician prescribes an appliance that will perform a particular function in the treatment of the patient. The prosthetist/orthotist then measures the patient carefully and accurately, using a ruler, tape measure, caliper, and other devices designed to measure the limbs and deformities. Often a plaster cast is made of the limb or deformity. Next the specialist designs the limb or brace to fit the individual patient according to the physician's prescription. Using a variety of materials, such as plastic, leather, wood, steel, and aluminum, the appliance is constructed and fitted to the patient. If necessary, the design is modified to achieve the most comfort and workability. The patient is then referred back to the physician for his approval. The prosthetist/orthotist is also responsible for servicing the appliance if it needs repairs or if it needs to be replaced.

The prosthetist/orthotist must be skilled in the use of the specialized tools and equipment used in fabricating, fitting, and aligning prostheses and orthoses and must also be skilled in the use of such standard tools as the drill press, bandsaw, disk sander, sewing machine, grinder, and buffer. The specialist must also know about new as well as old materials used in the trade. New plastics and new alloys have revolutionized the design and construction of braces and artificial limbs in recent years, and the prosthetist/orthotist must keep up with the latest developments in his field and know how to use them.

**A prosthetist teaching
students about the design
of an artificial limb.**

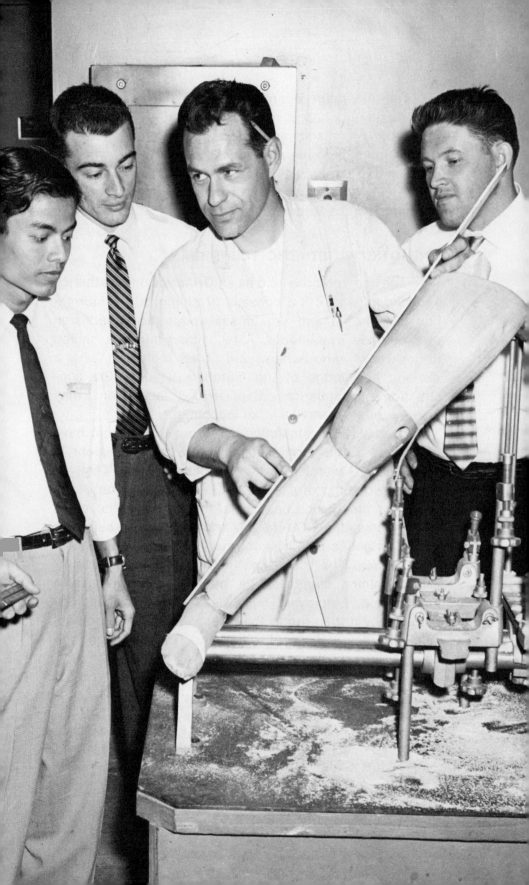

The American Board for Certification in Orthotics and Prosthetics has in recent years made moves to upgrade the profession and apply more well-defined and stricter job categories and qualifications. Those who are interested in the field should consider obtaining as much formal education as possible to insure success and advancement in the field in the coming years.

ORTHOTIC/PROSTHETIC TECHNICIAN

A person can enter the field as an **Orthotics** or **Prosthetics Technician,** whose job consists of aiding in the fabrication of orthoses and prostheses under the supervision of a certified practitioner. A technician must be skilled in the use of various hand and power tools and have a working knowledge of the materials used in the construction of appliances. Experienced technicians may be required to supervise other technicians.

To qualify as a technician, the candidate must have completed a tenth-grade education or the equivalent in the G.E.D. (General Educational Development) Test, as well as two years of experience in the fabrication of orthoses or prostheses before he/she can take the certifying examination. On-the-job training in a prosthetics and/or orthotics facility is the traditional way to become a technician. The U.S. Department of Labor has determined training standards for apprenticeship programs in this field. Employers must be willing to accept apprentices and then report their intentions to the Regional Office, Bureau of Apprenticeship and Training. Some col-

An orthotic device being used by a patient.

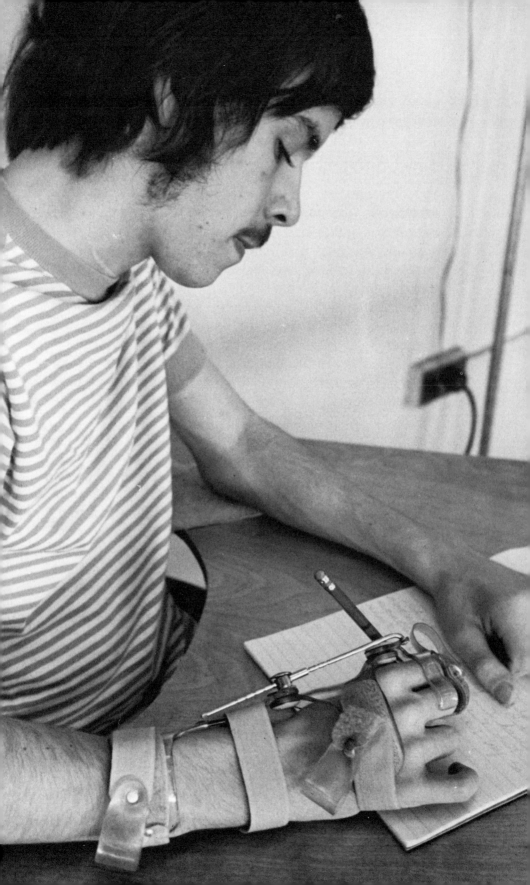

leges and hospitals around the country offer intensive year-long training courses for technicians.

ORTHOTIC/PROSTHETIC ASSISTANT

You may choose to enter the field as an **Orthotics** or **Prosthetics Assistant.** This job consists of aiding in the design and fitting of the orthoses or prostheses under the supervision of a practitioner. The assistant may be involved in making molds, taking measurements, and laying out and modifying the design. In the fitting process the assistant may be called on to make some of the parts and evaluate the fit while the patient is wearing the appliance.

To qualify as an assistant, you must obtain an associate in applied science degree on completion of a two-year program in prosthetics or orthotics at an accredited community college.

The standards are becoming stricter to enter the field as a practitioner in orthotics or prosthetics. Through 1979, candidates for certification must have an associate of arts degree in their intended field. After 1979 the basic educational requirement will be the completion of a four-year bachelor's degree program in prosthetics and orthotics, which combines both theory and practical experience. Applicants must furnish written recommendations from certified practitioners and physicians as proof of their clinical experience and training.

Those who complete a four-year apprenticeship, usually in a small shop or hospital, will also qualify to sit for the certifying examination. However, the recommended route is a college education.

The certifying examination, administered by the American Board for Certification in Orthotics and Prosthetics, Inc., consists of written, oral, and performance tests. Successful candidates are entitled to use the designation Certified Prosthetist, Certified Orthotist, or Certified Prosthetist-Orthotist.

Employment opportunities exist in hospitals, privately owned laboratories, and rehabilitation centers.

For further information contact:

American Orthotic and Prosthetic Association
1444 N Street, N.W.
Washington, D.C. 20005

In Canada contact:

Canadian Association of Prosthetists & Orthotists
1867 Alta Vista Drive
Ottawa, Ont.

The Canadian Board for Certification of Prosthetists & Orthotists
P.O. Box 8244
Ottawa, Ont. K1G 3H7

The Rehabilitation Counselor

Sandra Scones is a **Rehabilitation Counselor** at a service agency for those with impaired hearing. Between clients, phone calls to and from prospective employers, clients' family members, field trips, reports, staff meetings, and other tasks, her days are full with barely time to breathe.

A rehabilitation counselor (or vocational rehabilitation counselor) is one of the professionals in the rehab team who are working to restore the disabled or handicapped person to a level of efficiency that will enable him or her to lead a more satisfying and productive life.

His/her job is to evaluate the client's needs, desires, and capabilities—as gleaned from the reports of other team members, through tests he or she may administer, and through personal interviews with the client—and attempt to locate suitable employment opportunities. If the client's disability has left him or her unable to return to his or her former line of work, the rehabilitation counselor will help the patient explore alternative vocational opportunities. If additional education or training is needed, the counselor will locate places for these also.

In addition to vocational concerns, the rehabilitation counselor's job includes helping the client and his family adjust psychologically and socially to his or her changed condition. This would involve counseling for the client and sessions with the parents, husband or wife, and perhaps the children.

The counselor is a part of the rehabilitation process from its earliest stages through the post-discharge stage. During rehabilitation the counselor may be concerned about how the client is relating to the therapy and other aspects of the program to make sure the client is receiving the best possible benefits. Follow-up may last for as long as there is a need for the counselor's services provided the counselor's caseload permits. He or she may check periodically to see how a client is adjusting in a new employment situation and may serve as a resource person for the employer who may have questions or problems in employing someone with the client's particular disability.

In her position as rehabilitation counselor, Sandra handles a caseload of clients that includes all age groups from teen-agers to senior citizens. Working with teen-agers involves in-depth career education, individual exploration into vocations suitable to the person's abilities and personality, and counseling in education and training. She conducts an eight-week job workshop each summer for college graduates who are hearing impaired and works on job placements for them. Her goal is to find the right job for the particular client, rather than fit the client to the job. At times she functions as a mediator between employer and employees.

Working with hearing impaired people puts Sandra in the position of advocate for their cause, an educator to those ignorant of the causes and effects of hearing problems. She sees herself doing a good job if she can convince someone to have his or her hearing tested once every two years.

Her scheduled work hours are nine to five, with some flexibility. She sees from three to five clients a day in fifty-minute sessions and schedules field visits to prospective employers one day out of the week. One day stretches into the evening to fit in clients who are unable to come during the day.

Employment opportunities for rehabilitation counselors exist in state and federal divisions of vocational rehabilitation, voluntary agency service centers, sheltered workshops and rehabilitation centers, Veterans Administration facilities, drug abuse centers, and facilities for the emotionally disturbed, mentally retarded, and for public offenders.

At present there are no standard educational requirements for entering the field except a bachelor's degree from an accredited university. However, among applicants with only a four-year degree, employers tend to hire those with majors in the behavioral or social sciences or rehabilitation counseling. With the trend toward upgrading the professions, anyone interested in entering the field should plan to obtain a master's degree. If you major in rehabilitation counseling on the undergraduate level, you can work for a master's degree in social work, psychology, or another related field. If you major in social work, psychology, or education, you can pursue a master's degree in rehabilitation or vocational counseling. The curriculum should include such courses as medical aspects of rehabilitation, cultural and psychosocial aspects of disability, counseling techniques, survey of therapeutic care and rehabilitation, occupational and educational information. An internship is required in most courses of study.

Scholarships, grants-in-aid, and traineeship funds are available to qualified college graduates for graduate work in rehabilitation counseling.

For further information contact:

National Rehabilitation Association
1522 K Street, N.W.
Washington, D.C. 20005

American Rehabilitation Counseling Association
c/o American Personnel & Guidance Association
1607 New Hampshire Avenue, N.W.
Washington, D.C. 20009

The Speech Pathologist and the Audiologist

The **Speech pathologist** and/or **Audiologist** specializes in the communication problems that become evident in speech, language, and hearing. Speech pathologists are primarily concerned with speech and language disorders, while audiologists are concerned with hearing disorders. Since the speech and hearing systems are closely related, both physically and functionally, preparation for either field includes education in both areas.

[38]

Most speech pathologists work with children who suffer from speech impairment, such as stuttering, learning disabilities, hearing impairment, brain damage, mental retardation, and other problems.

Mary O'Connor works with children in a metropolitan-based agency that serves the hearing impaired. She has had among her clients a six-month-old infant. What could she do with a child so young? Fortunately the child's hearing impairment was diagnosed at an early age. A hearing aid was prescribed to augment what hearing ability the infant had. Mary's job was to educate the baby's ears and mind to the sounds he had missed before receiving the device. Because much of our ability to speak is the result of imitating what we hear, this procedure was crucial to the language development of the child. By this process the child develops an understanding of spoken words by associating certain sounds with certain objects and concepts. As the child matures, the concepts will become more abstract.

Another aspect of the therapy offered by the speech pathologist is the development of the mechanisms necessary for verbal expression, that is vocabulary, concepts, and visual and auditory memory. The client is taught (if necessary) to make the sounds, then the words, which then develop into phrases, sentences, and so on, until the shadings and complexities of normal spoken language have been achieved.

Parents are encouraged to sit in on such sessions with the child so that they can learn what to do at home to follow through with the therapy.

The pathologist also works to develop the remaining residual hearing by covering the visual clues, primarily the mouth, so that the child who is skilled in reading lips is forced to listen and discriminate between the sounds he or she hears.

Mary also teaches word-attack skills and remedial

skills necessary for reading. She sees clients on a one-to-one basis for one hour. She has six hours of therapy each day. In addition to planning and carrying out the therapy, her job includes administering tests to diagnose and evaluate the child's language ability, writing progress reports on each client, and attending periodic staff meetings.

Some speech pathologists choose to specialize in a particular area. Dr. Sam Donald works with aphasic adults in a Veterans Hospital. Aphasics are those people who have suffered neurological damage to the muscles used in speech through such illnesses as strokes, muscular dystrophy, or multiple sclerosis. Dr. Donald diagnoses the exact nature of the malfunctioning and plans and administers therapy to correct the condition as much as possible. Part of the therapy includes special exercises to reeducate the affected muscles. One stroke victim had such minimal control of his lower lip that he drooled constantly. Dr. Donald prescribed various exercises to strengthen his lower jaw as a step toward correcting the condition. Dr. Donald also works with patients who suffer swallowing problems following radiation therapy or surgery.

Ninety percent of Dr. Donald's time is spent with patients. The remaining 10 percent is devoted to research into the effectiveness of specific therapy and how the brain processes language.

The audiologist diagnoses hearing disorders by administering a variety of tests designed to determine a

**An audiologist working
with hearing deficient children.**

patient's hearing level and to identify the likely site of damage. He or she uses a machine that emits both tones and speech. The tones have different pitches, from very low to very high and from very soft to very loud. The audiologist registers the softest level at which the person can hear. The speech is used to determine how well the person is able to understand spoken speech, that is, to distinguish between the different sounds.

Part of the audiologist's work includes planning and carrying out therapy for children and adults whose hearing is impaired. He or she may teach lipreading to adults. The audiologist also prescribes a hearing aid when needed and schedules follow-up visits for periodic checkups. She or he conducts orientation classes for hearing impaired people who have just received hearing aids. She/he teaches them how to use the device, and how to adjust themselves to listening with the hearing aid. Because they are hearing unfamiliar sounds and because the sounds are loud and somewhat distorted, the clients have to learn how to interpret the sounds: They must learn how to listen through the hearing aid.

At institutions and agencies for the hearing impaired, the audiologist usually examines the clients and sends her/his reports to the speech pathologist. Thus she/he will work with infants also. Audiologist Marie Constant has a two-month-old infant to test. The child's parents believe she has a hearing problem and want to determine if this is the case. Marie will use toys that make noises and observe the baby's responses. She will transmit speech and calibrated tones through speakers and earphones to determine the level at which the child hears. The outcome of the test will determine if therapy and a hearing aid are needed.

To prepare for a career in speech pathology and

audiology, you must complete a four-year program leading to a bachelor of science or bachelor of arts degree in speech pathology or in a related field such as biology, psychology, or the physical sciences. In addition, you must complete an approved graduate program in speech pathology and audiology at an accredited university leading to a master of science degree. Those interested in becoming speech pathologists will concentrate their studies in the area of speech pathology, while those interested in becoming audiologists will concentrate their academic programs in audiology.

Some states require that speech pathologists and audiologists be licensed in order to practice. To be eligible for a license, the applicant must have a master's degree in speech pathology and/or audiology, pass the licensing examination, and have experience that satisfies the particular state requirements.

The American Speech and Hearing Association certifies clinical competence in this field. Certification can be obtained by graduates of approved programs who have, in addition, passed a national certifying examination.

Speech pathologists and audiologists are employed in hospitals, schools, special schools, and rehabilitation centers.

AUDIOMETRIST

An **Audiometrist** is a technician who is involved in screening hearing. He or she usually works under the supervision of an audiologist, administering certain tests and carrying out some of the treatment designed by the audiologist. Audiometrists may find employment in schools, hospitals, and clinics. The requirements for such a position consist of a bachelor's degree and one

An audiometrist (right) giving a hearing test.

year's experience in the speech and hearing department of a hospital or clinic that provides three months' work with the testing apparatus.

For further information contact:

American Speech and Hearing Association
9030 Old Georgetown Road
Bethesda, Md. 20014

In Canada contact:

Canadian Speech & Hearing Association
P.O. Box 1417
Ottawa, Ont.

The Orientation and Mobility Instructor

While other members of a rehabilitation team may work with a variety of disabilities, the **Orientation** and **Mobility Instructor** (also known as a Peripatologist and Orientation and Mobility Specialist) works only with the blind.

The title describes the job: teaching an individual how to orient to the environment and how to move from one place to another. An orientation and mobility instructor may work with all age groups: children as young as three years of age, teen-agers, adults, and the elderly. Their clients may be handicapped only visually or may suffer from several disabilities. The objective of the instruction, however, is the same for all, although the scope is adapted to the individual's capabilities and desires.

Instruction may begin with teaching how to use a sighted person as a guide, and how to use the arm and hands for protection against injury when moving about

[45]

indoors. When these skills are mastered, the next step is to teach the blind person how to use a cane for traveling. Proper use of this simple instrument greatly increases the visually impaired person's ability to be self-sufficient. The modern long lightweight aluminum cane with plastic tip on the end aids the visually impaired in surveying the terrain.

Dorothy Drayton was teaching eighteen-year-old Joan Collins how to use such a cane. She selected the hall of the service agency where she is employed as the work area. She guided Joan's hand into the proper grip on the handle and then moved her arm to extend directly in front of the midline of her body. Joan then tried to adopt the position herself. At first she held her arm too high, then too far from the side of her body. Each time Dorothy guided her arm to the proper position until she finally got the feel of it. Next Dorothy asked Joan to begin walking straight ahead, one foot in front of the other, using her wrist to move the cane to the left and then to the right in an arc in front of her. This motion provided Joan with a field of safety as far in front as the cane reached. She walked the length of the hall, using the intersection of the wall and floor as her line of reference, somewhat stiffly and self-consciously, but quite successfully. Dorothy congratulated her on her first attempt and continued practicing with her for another fifteen or twenty minutes. As Joan's confidence and skill in using the cane indoors increases, Dorothy will gradually widen her field of travel to stairs, elevators, throughout the building, and eventually outdoors, on public transportation and into stores.

An orientation and mobility instructor teaching a blind person to use a cane indoors.

Meanwhile, Dr. John Rocsin was in a room off the corridor with two teen-agers, instructing them in an aspect of sensory training, which is another part of orientation and mobility instruction. The goal of sensory training is to reeducate the remaining senses (i.e., hearing, touch, smell, kinesthesia, etc.). In each corner of the room, just beneath the ceiling, a speaker blared Latin music. As the music alternated from speaker to speaker, the students were asked to listen and gesture in the direction from which the music was coming. Being able to locate sounds is a necessary skill in orienting oneself to one's surroundings.

Dr. Rocsin utilizes fencing as a technique of sensory training. The method he developed aids in the reorganization of the sensorium (the entire sensory apparatus) by developing mental, physical, and emotional control and a wide range of other skills: coordination, motor memory, reflexes, quick judgment, gait, posture, locomotion, tactual perception in three-dimensional form, sound awareness, discrimination, concentration, attention-span, visualization, and imagination.

Dr. Rocsin then instructed his two students, Peggy Brown and David West, each about sixteen years old, to walk onto the rubber runner in the center of the room. Each held an épée and, once in position, were asked to touch swords. They made contact quite easily. They had to switch touch positions by disengaging and swinging the swords to the other side. Dr. Rocsin called out instructions as they moved their swords. Peggy advanced one step at a time while David retreated one step at a time. The object of the exercise was to touch swords each time, and they succeeded more often than not.

The work itself can be very demanding, both physically and emotionally. Instruction takes place on a one-to-one basis, which can lead to an intensity that is draining. The aim is to achieve a balance between being too protective and too detached. It requires outdoor as well as indoor work. The caseload can consist of six to eight students per course of instruction. In one agency students are seen five days a week for one hour a day. The orientation and mobility specialist assesses the needs and desires of each client and works out an individual instruction program, proceeding at the client's own pace.

Servicing canes is also part of the work. If a tip, handle, or entire cane needs replacing, the orientation and mobility specialist takes care of that.

New electronic devices designed to aid the visually impaired are constantly being developed and placed on the market. The O&M instructor must keep abreast of these new developments by taking courses that teach the use of these electronic aids.

Most orientation and mobility specialists are employed in agencies and schools for the blind and other institutions that may have the visually impaired persons among their population, such as nursing homes, hospitals, and public schools.

To become an orientation and mobility instructor requires either a four-year undergraduate degree or a master's degree, each from an accredited university. The program may include such courses as the psychological aspects of disability, medical aspects of disability, physiology and function of the eye, psychosocial aspects of blindness, and methods of communication with the blind. An important feature of training to become an O&M specialist is undergoing O&M instruction while blindfolded. Each student spends from fifty to one hundred and fifty hours under a blindfold in order to experience firsthand what it means to be blind. One master's program schedules this during the first of the two-semester sequence, with students working blindfolded two hours each day, five days a week, for fifteen weeks. An O&M instructor recalled that during this phase she experienced such frustration that she broke down and cried. The blindfolding enabled her to gain a deeper ability to empathize with her clients.

Also, each student is required to teach orientation and mobility to a small caseload of students and to serve an internship in an agency or a school servicing the visually handicapped.

Some universities offer a dual competency program. For example, upon completion of the master's program at the University of Northern Colorado's School of Special Education and Rehabilitation, the graduate is equipped to teach academic skills to visually handicapped children as well as orientation and mobility. Some undergraduate programs also offer dual competency.

Master's programs require a bachelor's degree from an accredited college in a discipline such as education, psychology, sociology, physical handicaps, or other related majors.

The American Association of Workers for the Blind certifies workers in the field. It offers Provisional and Permanent Certification. Permanent Certification is granted to an M.A.-trained O&M specialist if he or she applies within five years after receiving Provisional Certification, provides evidence of satisfactory full-time employment as an O&M specialist for at least three years after receiving Provisional Certification, and submits payment of the application fee. A baccalaureate-trained O&M specialist must present evidence of completion of an M.A. program in either special education or rehabilitation and of satisfactory full-time employment as an O&M specialist for at least three years after receiving Provisional Certification, and must also submit the application fee.

For further information contact:

American Association of Workers for the Blind
1511 K Street, N.W., Suite 637
Washington, D.C. 20005

In Canada contact:

The Canadian Council of the Blind
96 Ridout Street South
London, Ont. N6O 3X4

The Canadian National Institute for the Blind
1929 Bayview Ave.
Toronto, Ont. M4G 3E8

Other Therapies

The following sections describe vocations in the field of physical rehabilitation that are not always included in the core rehabilitation team. However, they are job categories that amplify and enhance any rehabilitation program. Directors of such programs are interested in viewing the patients they serve as complete entities composed of many aspects or parts. When one part is in a state of ill health, the other parts also are affected. Thus, a man who is partially paralyzed as a result of a stroke will no doubt suffer some emotional and psychological setbacks as well. The ideal, well-rounded, well-staffed rehabilitation program attempts to have among its personnel such professionals as music, art, and dance therapists who through their special expertise contribute to the total healing process.

Employment opportunities in such vocations are to a great extent dependent on the political climate of the times. If the government is favorable toward health, education, and public welfare, funds allocated to these areas will provide for the optimum level of staffing. If you will be entering the job market in the next five to ten years, keep abreast of the political atmosphere and its effects on employment opportunities in this field.

The Music Therapist

Artistic expression in musical form has in recent years been recognized for its therapeutic value. **Music Therapists** use their musical talents and capabilities in a prescribed manner, not to seek out and develop budding concert artists but for the therapeutic value of the process of making music. When the physician decides that music therapy would be beneficial, the music therapist confers with the physician and discusses with other members of the rehabilitation team the suggested course of treatment. She or he selects the musical activity and the methods of application, taking into account the patient's needs, capabilities, and interests.

The therapist employs a variety of musical techniques to improve or change the patient's mental outlook and aid in his or her rehabilitation. He or she organizes instrumental and vocal musical activities such as chorus, group, and solo singing, band and orchestra playing, and rhythm training. The therapist also arranges patients' concerts.

While working with patients in this manner, the musical therapist observes and studies their reactions for signs of progress or regression. He or she prepares periodic reports containing this information and submits them to the physician and other members of the rehabilitation team for their information.

[52]

Peter Johns entered the recreation room of the hospital where he is employed as a music therapist and began to wheel the piano into position. A few patients already were seated in chairs around the room. One was in a wheelchair. Peter sat down on the bench and began to play a medley of popular songs. Gradually the chairs filled as patients came in either on their own, escorted by nurses, or in wheelchairs. A few brought their own instruments, while others took the maracas, tambourines, and bongos offered by the volunteer worker. Within fifteen minutes the room was packed. As Peter played the songs that were requested, more people, drawn by the music, edged into the room.

Peter was continually alert to the response of the patients to the music. The group was mixed—Hispanic, Afro-American, Jewish, Irish, and other ethnic groups— and he included tunes of their respective cultures. He asked the volunteer if she had tried to put some instruments into the hands of two patients who appeared very self-absorbed. She replied that she had tried but they had refused. When a clarinetist among the patients joined in, a real jam session evolved, and the patients seemed caught up in the excitement and intensity of it all. It ended to wild applause.

In addition to conducting rhythm sessions such as these, Peter also leads a choral group in the hospital and plays music for a listening group. He also sees patients individually in his room down in the basement, where he is working with one patient to develop his singing ability as an aid to strengthening his lungs while he recovers from emphysema. Another patient, stricken with muscular dystrophy and unable to play the piano any more, took up singing as a mode of musical expression that was very helpful to him psychologically and also helped his breathing. For patients with a hand impairment, Peter uses the piano therapeutically to improve their manual dexterity.

[53]

A music therapist

Joan Moody, a music therapist at a service agency for the blind, works with the visually impaired by utilizing music to develop awareness of space and time, an awareness that is vital to their orientation and mobility.

The music therapist must be able to communicate verbally with patients to instruct them in their activities. The therapist must also be able to understand medical terminology and how to design a good therapy program.

Music therapy is a career possibility for the musically inclined person who might like to develop that inclination beyond the hobby point. Someone who aspires to the concert level of performance might also want to consider this rather unique way of utilizing his or her talent to serve others. However, the temperamental "artistic" types who have difficulty controlling their egos should shy away. Helping others requires a personality that can focus on the other person.

To qualify as a music therapist you must complete a four-year program leading to a bachelor's degree in music therapy that includes a six-month clinical internship. You can also major in a related field such as psychology or music education and obtain a master's degree in music therapy.

Music therapists are employed in physical disability hospitals, schools for the deaf, blind, and mentally retarded, nursing homes, rehabilitation centers, and psychiatric hospitals.

The National Association for Music Therapy establishes certain standards for registration. Although employment as a music therapist does not require registration by the NAMT, it is to the person's advantage to obtain as many professional credentials as possible.

For further information contact:

National Association for Music Therapy
P.O. Box 610
Lawrence, Kans. 66044

The Art Therapist

The **Art Therapist,** like the music therapist, utilizes his/
her medium of expression for its therapeutic value. While
the majority of art therapists appear to work with the
mentally ill and emotionally disturbed, their special ap-
proach is also used in the treatment and rehabilitation
of the physically handicapped and neurologically impaired.

Medical science is continually increasing its awareness of the extent to which the mind and body are in-
terrelated, and how the state of one affects the state of
the other. Therefore, the value of nonmedical therapeutic techniques is gaining, albeit slowly.

Art therapy is used as a mild form of exercise with
people suffering disabilities affecting the arms and hands.
It is used by cerebral palsy sufferers in this manner. Because art for many people is closely associated with
play, it can be used as a therapeutic form that is less
threatening than crafts, which carry a work connotation
and therefore invite judgments on performance.

One therapist described art as a vehicle through
which one's fantasies can be released. Thoughts and
anxieties related to one's physical condition can be put
in a form that can be seen and touched and therefore dealt
with and adjusted to in a more realistic way.

The value of art in instilling hope and a sense of
accomplishment is graphically displayed in the sight of
paraplegics painting with brushes held in their mouths
or toes and producing creditable works of art. For them,
art provided a stimulus to express emotional, intel-

lectual, and aesthetic sensitivity that might otherwise have remained locked inside.

Preparation for this field requires, first and foremost, a strong background in the media and techniques of art, such as painting, drawing, ceramics, and sculpture. A bachelor's degree with a major in art therapy, art, art education, or psychology is also necessary. Although those who major in art therapy and gain some clinical experience may be able to find some jobs available, the trend in rehabilitation services is toward upgrading and "professionalizing" each therapeutic discipline. It is therefore advisable to seek education and experience beyond the bachelor's degree in the form of a graduate program in art therapy leading to a master of arts, master of professional studies, or master of creative arts; a master's degree program in art education or psychology, with clinical training in art therapy; or completion of a certificate program in art therapy which includes clinical training.

The American Art Therapy Association sets the standards for acquiring professional status as an art therapist. Registration may not be necessary for employment, but it is advisable to work toward this goal. Applicants for registration must be active members of the association and must fulfill one of the following educational requirements: a master's degree in art therapy; graduate level clinical training or graduate level institute training, which is the equivalent of a master's degree in art therapy; or a master's or doctoral degree in another field plus experience in art therapy beyond the minimum experience requirements. Applicants must have completed a minimum of two thousand hours of supervised work experience and must show evidence of training and supervision with a Registered Art Therapist. In addition, applicants must produce evidence of a strong background in art. Candidates who meet these require-

[57]

ments and pass the qualifying examination are entitled to use the designation Registered Art Therapist (A.T.R.).

Art therapists work in schools for emotionally disturbed, mentally retarded, and brain-damaged children and in hospitals, community health centers, and private practice.

For further information contact:

American Art Therapy Association
3607 South Braeswood Boulevard
Houston, Texas 77025

The Dance Therapist

The **Dance Therapist,** also referred to as a Dance-Movement Therapist, uses movement in the treatment and rehabilitation of emotionally disturbed, neurologically impaired, and physically handicapped children and adults. He/she works with people who require special psychotherapeutic services because of behavioral, learning, perceptual, and/or physical disorders. Dance therapy is just beginning to gain grudging respect from other members of the rehabilitation team, so those interested in entering the field should be prepared to work and struggle hard to establish themselves.

John Clark is part of a rehabilitation team at a re-

A dance therapist

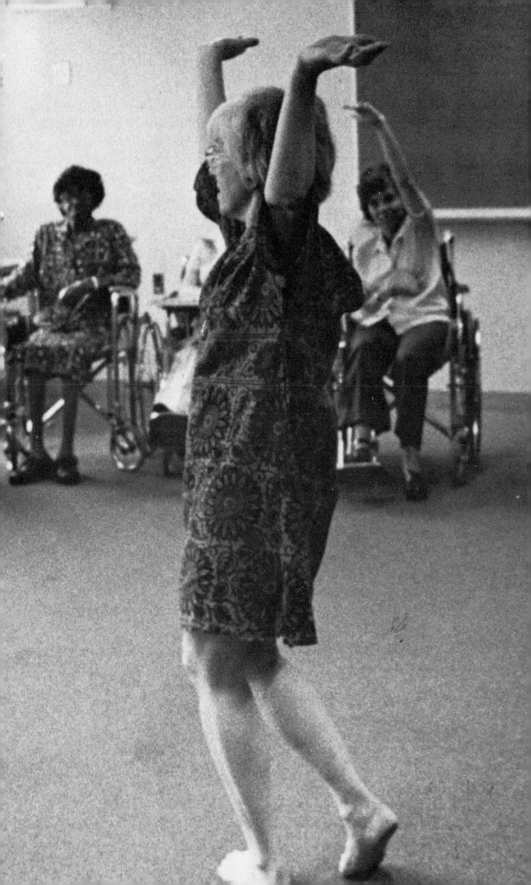

habilitation center attached to a large medical complex. Patients are referred to him with the physician's prescription. One person included in his caseload was a forty-five-year-old woman who had suffered a stroke. She developed a hesitant manner of walking and a fear of going out. She also had difficulty keeping her emotions straight, that is, she laughed when she wanted to cry and she cried when she wanted to laugh. John worked with her, teaching her to climb stairs in time to music. This, along with other prescribed movements, increased her stamina, improved her posture, and developed her confidence.

To develop coordination and to improve gait and to correct other problems in mobility caused by illness or injury, the dance therapist uses his knowledge of how the body moves in relation to space and rhythm. He/she also can help a patient learn to use an artificial limb.

Preparation for the field calls for an extensive background in dance plus a bachelor's degree in dance, dance education, psychology, or dance therapy. A master's degree in dance therapy is recommended but out of reach for many because there are fewer than ten such programs in the United States at the present time. A bachelor's or master's degree in special education, dance, psychology, or a related field may be sufficient if the person's dance background is very strong and if she/he enrolls in dance therapy training and a supervised clinical internship. Course work should include anatomy, movement observation, kinesiology, movement behavior, psychology of small groups, and psychology of the handicapped.

The American Dance Therapy Association provides registration for qualified members. Applicants must have completed 3,640 hours of salaried dance therapy employment and meet other criteria of clinical practice, training, education, and experience that includes work in choreographing, performing, and teaching dance. Those who become certified may use the title Dance Therapist Registered and may engage in private practice and supervise other dance therapists.

Dance therapists are employed in psychiatric hospitals, clinics, day care centers, residential and community mental health centers, rehabilitation centers, correctional facilities, and in private and group practice.

For further information contact:

American Dance Therapy Association
1000 Century Plaza, Suite 216E
Columbia, Md. 21044

Index

[63]